DO YOU REALLY WANT TO MEET
A CAPE BUFFALO?

WRITTEN BY CARI MEISTER   ILLUSTRATED BY DANIELE FABBRI

Amicus Illustrated and Amicus Ink
are imprints of Amicus
P.O. Box 1329
Mankato, MN 56002
www.amicuspublishing.us

Library of Congress Cataloging-in-Publication Data
Meister, Cari, author.
 Do you really want to meet a cape buffalo? /
by Cari Meister ; illustrated by Daniele Fabbri.
    pages cm. — (Do you really want to meet...?)
 Summary: "A child goes on an African safari and
observes the behavior of Cape buffalo in the wild
as they defend their herd"— Provided by publisher.
 Audience: K to grade 3.
 ISBN 978-1-60753-738-0 (library binding)
 ISBN 978-1-60753-842-4 (ebook)
 ISBN 978-1-68152-006-3 (paperback)
 1. African buffalo–Juvenile literature. I. Fabbri,
Daniele, 1978– illustrator. II. Title.
 QL737.U53M43 2016
 599.64'2–dc23   2014036518

Editor   Rebecca Glaser
Designer   Kathleen Petelinsek

Printed in the United States of America at
Corporate Graphics in North Mankato, Minnesota.

HC 10 9 8 7 6 5 4 3 2 1
PB 10 9 8 7 6 5 4 3 2 1

ABOUT THE AUTHOR

Cari Meister is the author of more than 120 books for
children, including the *Tiny* (Penguin Books for Young
Readers) series and *Snow White and the Seven Dogs*
(Scholastic, 2014). She lives in Evergreen, Colorado, with
her husband John, four sons, one horse, and one dog.
You can visit Cari online at *www.carimeister.com*.

ABOUT THE ILLUSTRATOR

Daniele Fabbri was born in Ravenna, Italy, in 1978. He
graduated from Istituto Europeo di Design in Milan, Italy,
and started his career as a cartoon animator, storyboarder,
and background designer for animated series. He has
worked as a freelance illustrator since 2003, collaborating
with international publishers and advertising agencies.

L ook at that strange creature. See
its big horns and cow-like eyes?

It's not a cow. It's a Cape buffalo!

What? You want to see one up close? Cape buffalo are more dangerous than lions. Cape buffalo kill over 200 people a year in Africa.

You still *really* want to meet a Cape buffalo? Okay. Pack your suitcase. It's time to go on safari in Africa. Don't forget sunscreen and a hat. The sun in Africa can be intense.

It won't be hard to find Cape buffalo here.
Cape buffalo live in large herds—sometimes
up to 2,000 buffalo live in a group.

Time to explore. Beware! You never want to sneak up on a buffalo. If you do, you might startle it. Then it will charge, aiming its large pointed horns right at you! It won't eat you (buffalo are herbivores), but it might gore you to death.

Keep your distance! That is one huge buffalo! Cape buffalo can weigh up to 1900 pounds (860 kg). So if he doesn't want to eat you—why would he attack?

So you do not kill *him*. Cape
buffalo are one of the most
hunted animals in Africa. In
their minds, all humans could
be dangerous—they don't
know if you are a hunter or not.

Phew! It looks like another threat has arrived—LIONS! Those lions are stalking the herd. They want to grab a baby buffalo for lunch. The buffalo push their calves to the center of the herd. This makes it harder for the lions to snag one.

The baby buffalo is safe.
But, wait. Why is that buffalo
charging the lion pride?

It's going after a cub!

Cape buffalo are known to retaliate against lions by picking up cubs and throwing them high into the air. Sometimes, the cubs are killed on impact.

Here's another herd. Cape buffalo sure have some interesting friends. Do you see the oxpecker birds? They help buffalo by picking off bugs to eat and by cleaning out their noses. Tasty.

Aachoo! It looks like you might need an oxpecker to clean your nose. There sure are a lot of biting flies around here! If they start to drive you crazy, you can do what the buffalo do.

Cover yourself in mud! It protects your skin AND it helps you stay cool. Do you want to get closer?

No? Smart choice. It is much safer to watch Cape buffalo from afar than to meet them face-to-face.

WHERE DO CAPE BUFFALO LIVE?

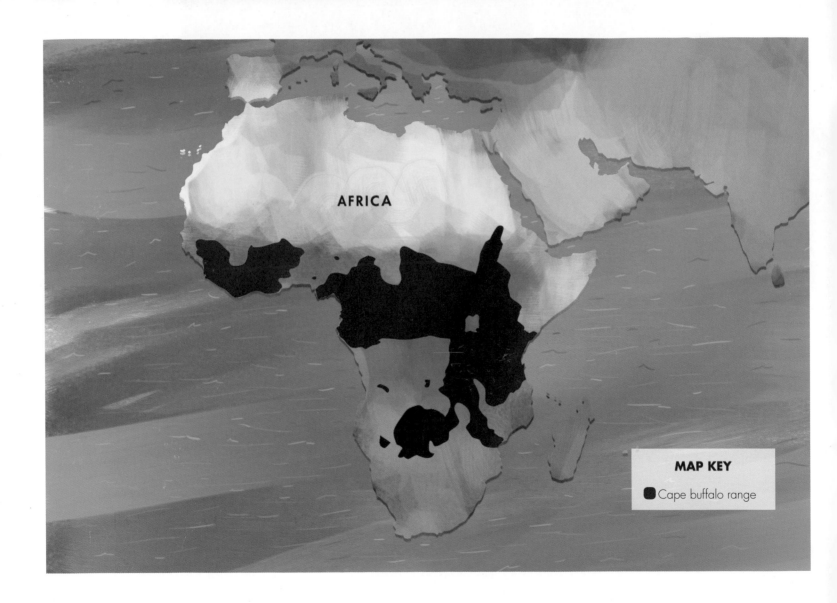

AFRICA

MAP KEY

● Cape buffalo range

GLOSSARY

gore To pierce with a horn, often over and over again.

herbivore An animal that eats only plants.

oxpecker A bird that lives on other animals and eats insects from its skin.

pride A group of lions that live and hunt together.

retaliate To seek revenge.

safari An exploring vacation, often to look for animals. "Safari" means "long journey" in the African language Swahili.

READ MORE

Gibbs, Maddie. African Buffalo.
New York: PowerKids Press, 2011.

Owings, Lisa. **The Cape Buffalo**.
Minneapolis: Bellwether Media,
2012.

Rustad, Martha. **African Animals**.
North Mankato, Minn.: Capstone
Press, 2014.

Stewart, Melissa. **Deadliest Animals**.
Washington, D.C.: National
Geographic, 2011.

WEBSITES

African Buffalo | Arkive
*http://www.arkive.org/african-buffalo/syncerus-caffer/
video-na00.html*
Watch videos and see photos of Cape buffalo in the wild.

African Buffalo | The Animal Files
*http://www.theanimalfiles.com/mammals/
hoofed_mammals/buffalo_african.html*
Read more about the African Buffalo

African Cape Buffalo: Sea World Animal Bytes
*http://seaworld.org/en/animal-info/animal-bytes/
mammals/african-cape-buffalo/*
Get all the basic facts about the Cape buffalo.
This is a good resource for reports.

*Every effort has been made to ensure that these websites are appropriate for
children. However, because of the nature of the Internet, it is impossible to
guarantee that these sites will remain active indefinitely or that their contents
will not be altered.*